Inspiring Unconditional Love

Reflections from the Heart

By

Harold W. Becker

White Fire Publishing

Inspiring Unconditional Love
Reflections from the Heart

By Harold W. Becker

Published by:
White Fire Publishing
Tampa, Florida
www.whitefirepublishing.com

Cover Design and Interior Layout: John T. Goltz

Library of Congress Control Number: 2010929422

ISBN: 978-0-979046-03-2

First Printing: June 2010
Printed in the USA on acid free paper

The journey of a lifetime begins with the first step; and when that step is taken with unconditional love as our intention, the adventure is assured to be filled with joy. Our heart knows the dreams we seek to manifest and is our ever present guide along the way. We need only stay present in the moment and be aware of these intuitive impulses that unfold our path naturally.

We are brilliantly creative beings and our potential is magnificent beyond measure. By simply staying balanced in harmony and love, we can accomplish our greatest desires that benefits and expands the very essence of life itself.

Open your heart in this moment and release your treasure of love. Share your precious gifts of compassion and you will encourage others to remember theirs. Together we make a difference through unconditional love.

Harold W. Becker

Inspiring Unconditional Love

Reflections from the Heart

The beauty of love is all around us
when we have an open heart.

Today is a new day and a fresh
opportunity to love unconditionally.

Love begins with me - now there is a
difference we can each make.

Unconditional love is the answer to the question.

Love life simply as it is and allow
the beauty to reveal itself.

Life is such a wonderful adventure.

Love changes everything yet
love itself never changes.

Spread some unconditional love
around the world today.

Love without condition and see
how your reality changes.

Giving in to fear is easy; loving unconditionally
is easier once you make the choice.

When we celebrate and love ourselves unconditionally, we instantly understand and embrace everyone and everything around us.

Unconditional love is an unlimited way of being.

Truly trust your heart and amazing things will happen in your life.

Patience and trust are two main qualities of unconditional love.

Nothing is ever what it appears to be since love resides within each experience, sometimes obvious and other times seemingly invisible.

Express the real you that you are.

Unconditional love is a journey
without beginning or end.

Loving unconditionally takes courage,
giving into fear does not.

To know love is to be love.

Follow your heart and you will never get lost.

Be fully present in the moment
and you are instantly free.

Letting go allows energy to flow.

Our body is our temple and our home.

Life was different yesterday yet love remains the same today.

Every moment of every day is a new beginning.

Peace prevails and so does love.

The Universe is full of fun surprises.

When the "ah ha" moment becomes
the "ha ha" moment, we are free.

When we let go of yesterday, anything is possible.

Love is the universal language of the heart.

Just for today let love guide the way.

When the whole world is your playground, things get interesting.

When we accept ourselves just for who we are, we accept other people just for who they are.

Forgiveness is the exquisite healer in all of us.

Balance is the key to well being.

Life is a gift.

When you see yourself as whole and complete, you see it in all others too.

Listen to your heart - you may be surprised by what you hear.

Love dissolves fear.

Breathe and allow life to be what it is.

When we honor ourselves, we honor others.

Inner harmony provides balance and clear action.

There is beauty in every moment when
we see through the eyes of our heart.

Laughter is a gift that heals.

Love - the more you give, the more you receive.

Chapters close, yet the heart knows
that the book goes on forever.

Breathe in and experience this moment.

Let unconditional love be your walking meditation today and watch what happens.

Anything is possible with an open heart and open mind.

Dreams of the heart do come true.

Letting go and allowing is actually easier than holding on to what no longer serves.

Freedom already exists in the heart.

It is important to be and speak our truth; we just need to make sure that it is really ours.

To know thyself is to trust thyself.

When we open our heart we also open our mind.

When we are present and aware, the next step we take creates a whole new adventure.

Celebrate who you are - a magnificent being filled with love.

Embrace change in the outer with the awareness of love within.

With unconditional love, all things are whole and complete.

Life is a never ending adventure and love is our constant companion.

Today is a new beginning, what shall we create through love?

Maintain inner harmony no matter how the winds may blow.

Unconditional love is actually very simple and easy, once you choose to let it flow.

To truly know love simply ask, what am I attached to and why? Then let go.

Now is the time to inspire others
with your unconditional love.

Unconditional love is our universal
language - heart to heart.

Love is always present.

Speak from your heart and you change the world.

By focusing on unconditional
love, we become love.

In this present moment, imagine the infinite
possibilities and then choose the one you love.

Patience is both a virtue and an act of self love.

Be the cause of love today, just because.

When we are quiet and still, we
become aware of love.

Life flows naturally when you trust your heart.

Never hesitate to share your love.

Be courageous and choose to
love unconditionally.

What you wish for others through your thoughts and feelings is also what you wish for yourself.

Angels live to love, so what are you waiting for?

Create from the heart with harm to none.

You are a brilliant, creative and imaginative being - what will you choose to manifest today?

Smiling is an easy way to share your love.

Conscious thinking allows us to have conscious choice.

Be YOUR truth, not the suggestions and assumptions of others - your heart knows the difference.

Unconditional love unites our individual uniqueness.

What we imagine, we eventually create.

Unconditional love simplifies things that appear complex.

With trillions of stars in billions of galaxies, it is a wonder that we remain so human in our perspective.

Simply be, no matter what.

Love expresses to us and through us.

Love is present everywhere you go today and with all those you encounter - allow it to reveal itself.

You are infinitely more than you perceive yourself to be.

Love for no reason and you will have infinite reason to love.

Hugs and smiles are simple ways to love unconditionally all through the day.

As you share your love freely, others may realize they have love to share.

When you open your heart, you
open your eyes to a new reality.

Trust the wisdom that comes from your heart.

Loving others unconditionally begins
with loving yourself unconditionally.

Your personal choice to love
unconditionally changes the world.

As we love life, life itself expands in love.

Unconditional love unifies and
celebrates diversity.

Love the ONE you are!

Unconditional love reveals who we are at the center of our being.

Unconditional love simplifies life.

From the very first cell we have the potential to love unconditionally.

Be your own best friend and you will be a friend to the world.

Do not be afraid of life, embrace it with love and fear will disappear.

Even when others choose fear you
can be the one to choose love.

To know true love is to know true peace.

All life interconnects to all life.

Love and peace... one becomes the other.

Simply choose to love unconditionally - it is the one choice you will never regret.

Radiate your light today and watch the darkness disappear.

Be alive and present right now and notice the simple beauty all around you.

In the seeming complexity of life, be the simplicity of love.

I love you unconditionally. Yes, YOU! Feels good, doesn't it?

Keep life simple, you will enjoy it more.

Create from the heart and the adventure will be more spontaneous and grand.

Life becomes really interesting when we become aware of ourselves as the observer and the participant.

Love is the best place to begin your next step.

Wherever we go, there we are.
Wherever we are, there is love.

Embrace your grandness.

Your willingness to love changes everything and everyone.

Heart to heart we build a new world.

When we know the love within, there is nothing to seek... there is only to be.

Love in the heart brings peace to the mind.

Beautiful you; thank you for being on earth today - you are making a difference.

When you love, you remember who you truly are.

The beauty of love is eternal in the moment.

Joy in the heart leads to peace in the world.

The opportunity to express love is
present in every moment.

Our heart reminds us, "I am perfection perfecting itself."

The world is more beautiful today with your personal presence of love.

Loving unconditionally is easy, living with limitations and fear is much more difficult.

Love knows no bounds, it simply keeps expanding.

You are more than just a physical being, you are the presence of love.

The love in your heart is more precious when shared.

You are loved beyond measure.

Appreciate life and you will realize the gentle companionship of love.

Unconditional love embraces duality as one.

Ascend in love and a new world is born.

With each breath, love flows to you and through you in an endless stream.

The beauty of the day is in the heart of the moment.

Amidst the chaos of a changing world
is the harmony of love in the heart.

Make everyday a day of love and you
will be filled with loving memories.

Love and appreciate yourself unconditionally
and the world will know love by your example.

Infuse love into every thought, feeling, word, deed and action and you will experience a new world.

Think with your heart and feel with your mind.

You are beautiful, courageous, wise, and above all - the grand embodiment of love.

When we maintain harmony under all circumstances we allow our love to flow.

It all starts with unconditional self acceptance and love - if you don't love yourself, how can you truly love another?

Explore your heart today and find a new world filled with love.

Life is already filled with love, enjoy it.

What we have within, we give out. What we give out returns to us in full measure. The circle of love is complete.

Love is ever present; we only pretend at times that it is not here.

Someone in your world needs a loving hug today, give it freely and unconditionally and watch what happens.

Wherever there is gratitude there is love.

We are all angels disguised as humans!

Appreciation for all that has been and presently is brings joy of anticipation in all that will yet be.

Smiles are hugs from the heart.

Love is who we are; everything else is the illusion when we forget who we are.

Whether we choose to love or not,
love remains ever present.

The language of love is laughter.

Being kind, gentle and loving to yourself leads
to a gentler, kinder and more loving world.

The simplest gift we can ever offer is unconditional love from our heart.

Unconditional love is who you are behind the mask of who you think you are.

Reveal the joy of your soul by dancing to the tune of love in your heart.

An open heart and an open mind allow
us to embrace life with open arms.

Whatever you choose in each moment let
unconditional love be your guiding intention.

Love discovers the essence of creation
and the joy of potential.

We cannot change anyone yet we can love everyone unconditionally.

You can choose a path of joy just as easy as one of struggle; both will get you to your destination.

When we share our love, we give the present of our presence.

You light up the world with your love.

Expand your love today by sharing it with others.

Have no fear love is already here.

It is easy to go with the flow when
you are on a river of love.

Miracles are simply love in action. Be the miracle.

Unconditional love reveals life's exquisite beauty.

Each moment we remember love we forget fear.

When we love unconditionally, every moment is a new beginning.

Listen to your own heart beat and you will understand the source of love.

Love is a freedom known only
by those who share it.

Unconditional love is an intimate and
universal awareness of our true self.

When we are at peace with ourselves,
we are at peace with the world.

Love today and tomorrow your
past will be filled with love.

If you don't see love in the mirror of
life, doubt and fear are still present...
let go and love will flow.

Acceptance, allowance and compassion
for self and others are indications of
unconditional love in action.

Trust yourself and your own wisdom
and life will respond accordingly.

When we keep love simple, we simply love.

Expand your vocabulary to include unconditional
love and watch how your reality changes.

Unconditional love reveals the grace
and dignity inherent in life.

Peace and love are the most precious and
priceless commodities in our world that can
neither be bought nor sold… simply shared.

Change is inevitable while the
heart of love remains eternal.

Your presence of love is vital to the world.

Love was, love is and love will forever be who you are at the center of your being.

Be an avatar of love by expressing unconditionally from your heart.

Fear is nothing more than the illusion that we are somehow separate from love.

The world needs and wants love more than anything else - so let us be the ones to provide it.

You are a magnificent presence of love embodied in our world right now - thank you for being here!

We live to love just as we love to live.

Open your heart and experience
a grander view of the world.

Life with love creates an ever changing
landscape of experiences and potential.

This planet does not need more visions of desperation, fear, doubt and hate - it requires unconditional love to restore its natural beauty.

When we remain harmonious, wisdom flows in from the heart and dispels any doubt or fear.

The presence of love is already within, simply let it flow.

Joy, by its own nature, is an outward and upward movement of energy.

As you generously share the love in your heart, you are naturally fulfilling your life purpose.

Unconditional love is an incredibly intimate and personal journey shared with everyone.

When we feel separate from love,
simply step back until the love that
is present becomes obvious.

When we are fully present, love is in the air
we breathe, the thoughts we have, the hands
we hold, and the path we walk upon.

The heart knows true abundance and
flows continuously and unconditionally.

Imagine love and love will be the image and the experience.

Always be brave, courageous and outrageous with your love.

Each of us holds the key of love to unlock our collective potential.

Let your heart be your guide and
your mind be your companion.

Love often whispers through our heart
while nature sings it out loud.

There has never been a better moment than
right now to love yourself unconditionally.

If you wait for another to love you,
you miss the joy of true love.

Unconditional love is the conscious
awareness of the love that you are.

The wisdom of your heart is the only
guru you will ever need or want.

When we understand who we are,
we recognize everyone else.

While the mind often wanders,
the heart remains in love.

For much of my life fear was my companion
and motivator, and then unconditional
love came and inspired me.

Love knows all things as love while
fear only knows itself.

When you choose love you inspire others to love.

Forget who you were and instead remember
who you are... a magnificent being of love.

The love you seek never left.

The more you share your love the
more love you have to share.

Creating life with love manifests a very different
reality than one based on fear and doubt.

To love and appreciate life is to enjoy the amazing potential that is within and around us every moment.

The beauty of your life is reflected in the story of love that you share with others.

We touch the world with love right where we are.

Simply love unconditionally and there will be no room for fear or doubt.

Let your love shine as brilliant as the noonday sun.

We can approach life as a struggle or with joy; the choice is ours in each moment.

The one who truly knows unconditional love is indeed very lucky.

Although life is an intensely personal journey, we are forever surrounded by loving friends.

With unconditional love we see the bigger picture of life with greater clarity.

Listen to your heart and hear
the wisdom of eternity.

If you declare something wrong, it
doesn't necessarily make you right.

Fear and doubt are based in past and future
while love and joy are present in the moment.

Compassion lifts the energy of any situation into its natural state of unconditional love.

Peace is an inner quiet solitude which knows no bounds.

An expression of kindness can heal the hardest heart and repair the emotional pain of ages.

Inspiration is the timely awareness of opportunity.

Each of us has a special gift to share with the rest of humanity - it is the gift of love.

The rich tapestry of life weaves its love in every atom and allows us to play in the vast field of infinite oneness.

To love ourselves is to forgive ourselves; to forgive ourselves is to find the pearl within.

You are an amazing being filled with love, all else is a temporary illusion.

Unconditional love is the universal power that unites us and brings meaning to life.

Let us open our hearts and allow the dance of love to permeate all life.

Love and peace are qualities we cultivate through the choices we make.

When we realize our potential to love unconditionally, we transform ourselves and the planet at the same time.

Unconditional love shifts our perspective from shame, humiliation and intimidation to respect, dignity and encouragement.

Embrace yourself and you embrace the universe.

When we remember that love is the answer, we forget there ever was a question.

When we have harmony in our feelings and thoughts we are able to experience unconditional love.

Each time we take a deep breath, we give our heart a hug.

It is the unconditional kindness you show towards yourself and others that makes love tangible.

To choose to love unconditionally is both simple and courageous.

Let unconditional love be your focus today and you will observe a whole new reality.

Love is eternally yours and you are forever love itself.

We honor our precious earth
with gratitude and love.

As you expand and share your love you make
a world of difference right where you are.

Connect with the wisdom of your heart
and life flows naturally and easily.

Love expresses itself in infinite ways when your heart and mind are open to the possibilities.

When your intention is to love unconditionally, your life becomes a reflection of that same love.

Love isn't something we do, it is who we are.

Precious, beautiful, courageous and loving
- now do you remember who you are?

As you take each breath and step today,
simply know "love begins with me."

Our love is our gift to the world.

Whatever you desire in life, let it come from your heart and be filled with love.

It all begins within.

The love is universal, the choice is individual.

Unconditional love is priceless and forever free.

The mind contemplates a limited love where an open heart expresses unconditional love.

The love you seek is within and the love you share is the reflection to others of its source.

We are one love with an infinite
diversity of expression.

Whatever you may think you know is
insignificant to the grandness of who you are.

The joy you feel comes from the love you share.

Those with a courageous heart quietly guide others through the strength and wisdom of love.

In the silence of love one hears the music of eternity.

The natural rhythm of life is through the heartbeat of love.

Be true to yourself and let your light shine!

Your smile reminds others that love is present.

Whenever two greet in unconditional
love their reflection becomes one.

Love begins right where you are.

Open your heart and you will be amazed
with the treasure you find there.

With love as your guide you walk the
journey of one along a path of many.

The beauty of life is felt as the
pure essence of love.

Radiate your love and you
magnetically attract more.

To forgive without condition or expectation is
to bestow dignity upon every experience.

Within the stillness of the mind one can hear the voice of love.

Compassion embraces what judgment separates.

Integrity is found in one who follows the wisdom of their heart.

We come into this world filled with limitless potential so that we may know that love is infinite in its expression.

It takes courage to embrace your potential and wisdom to know what that is.

When we are aware of love there is never a more perfect moment than right now.

A loving heart cultivates a serene
mind and a life of joy.

To love unconditionally is to recognize the
unlovable and unloved as lovable and loving.

You are here right now for only one true
purpose and that is to share your love.

About the Author

Harold W. Becker has dedicated his life to understanding, living and sharing unconditional love. In 1990 he formed his consulting company, Internal Insights, and in 2000 he founded the non-profit, The Love Foundation, Inc., with the mission of "Inspiring people to love unconditionally."

In his desire to touch the world with this timeless message of love, Harold conceived Global Love Day, an international celebration of humanity, held annually each May 1st.

He is the author of several additional books including, *Internal Power: Seven Doorways to Self Discovery*, *Unconditional Love – An Unlimited Way of Being* and *Unconditional Love Is... Appreciating Aspects of Life* and wrote and hosted his own PBS special program entitled, *Unconditional Love – A Guide to Personal Freedom* available on DVD.

Harold has an MBA and enjoys bringing his inspirational and motivational vision into every facet of his life including his business activities, writing, speaking, seminars and consulting. Blending incredible insight and intuition with humor, compassion and kindness, he encourages people to love unconditionally.

You can reach Harold through the following web sites:
www.internalinsights.com
www.thelovefoundation.com
www.globalloveday.com
www.whitefirepublishing.com

www.ingramcontent.com/pod-product-compliance
Lightning Source LLC
LaVergne TN
LVHW020648100826
845148LV00012B/2381